Searchlight BOOKS

Future Tech

The Future of Food

Kevin Kurtz

Lerner Publications ◆ Minneapolis

Lerner Publications Company
an imprint of Lerner Publishing Group, Inc.
241 First Avenue North
Minneapolis, MN 55401 USA

For reading levels and more information, look up this title
at www.lernerbooks.com.

Main body text set in Adrianna Regular.
Typeface provided by Chank.

Library of Congress Cataloging-in-Publication Data

Names: Kurtz, Kevin, author.
Title: The future of food / Kevin Kurtz.
Description: Minneapolis : Lerner Publications, [2021] | Series: Searchlight books -
    future tech | Includes bibliographical references and index. | Audience: Ages 8—11 |
    Audience: Grades K–1 | Summary: "As Earth's human population grows, scientists
    and farmers must find new ways to create more food with less space. Learn about
    the challenges farmers face, the future of the meat industry, and much more."—
    Provided by publisher.
Identifiers: LCCN 2019045785 (print) | LCCN 2019045786 (ebook) |
    ISBN 9781541597303 (library binding) | ISBN 9781728400822 (ebook)
Subjects: LCSH: Food security—Juvenile literature. | Food supply—Juvenile literature. |
    Sustainable agriculture—Juvenile literature. | Food—Environmental aspects—Juvenile
    literature.
Classification: LCC HD9000.5 .K865 2021 (print) | LCC HD9000.5 (ebook) | DDC
    338.1/9—dc23

LC record available at https://lccn.loc.gov/2019045785
LC ebook record available at https://lccn.loc.gov/2019045786

Manufactured in the United States of America
1-47834-48274-12/30/2019

Contents

Chapter 1

FOOD CHALLENGES

In the future, you may eat chicken for dinner that grew in a laboratory. The lettuce in your salad could come from a farm that floats on the ocean. Your dessert might be 3D-printed just for you to include nutrients your body needs.

It takes a lot of time, work, and space to produce the food we eat.

Crop farms take up a lot of land and require huge, expensive machines to produce food.

The future of food will likely bring some big changes. To understand them, you should know where food comes from. Just about everything we eat comes from farms. When you enjoy a meal at a restaurant, the meat in your hamburger comes from cows raised by farmers. The flour in your bun and the potatoes in your fries come from crop farms. Even your soda pop has ingredients from farms. The sweetness in most sodas comes from corn syrup.

More Mouths to Feed

Around eight billion people live on Earth, and farmers provide food for almost all of them. About 19 million square miles (49 million sq. km) of Earth's land are used for farming. That much land would cover North America, South America, and Australia combined!

THE AVERAGE AMERICAN EATS ABOUT 1 TON (0.9 T) OF FOOD EACH YEAR.

With traditional farming methods, farmers will need even more land to produce enough food for Earth's growing human population.

The world's population keeps growing. By 2050, farmers will probably have to feed about ten billion people. But not much land is left that could easily convert to farmland. And climate change is affecting some of the land we use to farm. Some places are wetter or drier than they were in the past.

Farms have a big impact on the environment. Each acre of farmland takes away habitat from wildlife. Fertilizers, pesticides, and even cow burps are sources of environmental pollution. The more we farm, the harder it is for wild plants and animals to survive.

Farmers spray chemicals on fields to kill pests and weeds, allowing crop plants to produce more food.

These are big challenges, but farmers and scientists are working to overcome them. They are figuring out how to feed more people with less damage to the environment. They already have some amazing ideas.

Chapter 2

LET'S TALK ABOUT MEAT

It takes a lot of animals to feed the world's meat lovers. Billions of cows, pigs, sheep, turkeys, and other livestock live on farms. The world's twenty-three billion chickens weigh more than all the other birds on the planet combined. The chickens don't live long, though. We eat about sixty-five billion of them a year. All these livestock cause two big problems.

Many chickens raised for meat spend their entire lives inside a farm building.

First, the animals create about 15 percent of the greenhouse gases released into the atmosphere by human activity. Greenhouse gases trap heat and cause Earth's climate to change. A lot of the gases come from the planet's one billion cows. Cow burps and farts contain a powerful greenhouse gas called methane.

IN 2019, US FARMERS RAISED MORE THAN THIRTY MILLION BEEF COWS.

▼

Cows on farms eat mostly hay, grass, and grains such as corn and oats.

Raising livestock also requires more land than growing food crops. Farmers need to produce corn, soy, and other plants to feed the livestock. The animals eat about 7 pounds (3.1 kg) of grain for every 2 pounds (0.9 kg) of meat they produce.

Many people think we should use more of our precious farmland to raise plants instead of livestock. But some people love meat. How do we produce meat while dealing with the problems livestock cause?

It can be difficult to tell the difference between a plant-based burger (*pictured*) and a burger made from cow meat.

Meatless Meat

You're at a restaurant and order a burger. It looks like beef. It tastes like beef. It feels like beef in your mouth. But none of the ingredients come from animals. Businesses such as Impossible Foods and Beyond Meat make plant-based "meat." Their hamburger patties are made mostly of plants such as coconuts, peas, bamboo, and beets.

Meat made from plants is better for the environment than livestock is. The production of plant-based meat creates fewer greenhouse gases and needs less land. Plant-based meat and dairy companies are designing chicken, seafood, cheese, and even ice cream products. Soon most of your meat and dairy foods could come from plants.

Food scientists recommend eating a broad range of fruits and vegetables to stay healthy. Plant-based meat can help people get the nutrients they need.

The Future of Ew!

An animal exists that could provide humans with plenty of nutritious food and lessen our impact on the environment. The problem is, many people think eating bugs is gross. People around the world already eat more than nineteen hundred insect species. Insects need much less land to grow than larger livestock, so they could feed the world on fewer acres. More farms are raising insects, and many people already think bugs are delicious. Someday, you may too.

Fried corn dough topped with refried beans, worms, grasshoppers, and beetles

Lab Meat

Labs could be another future meat source. Businesses are working on real chicken meat that doesn't come from a chicken. Scientists take stem cells from parts of the animals that we want to eat. Stem cells easily multiply and grow in a lab. Eventually, enough of the cells make a steak, a chicken breast, or other kinds of meat.

Scientists are still working to produce meat in a lab that looks and tastes like meat from an animal.

Pigs in factory farms live on hard floors with little room to move around. Growing meat in labs would allow fewer pigs to live in such conditions.

Lab-grown meat has advantages over livestock. When an animal is killed for food, bones, lungs, and other parts we don't eat are discarded. All the meat grown in a lab can be eaten, and the process doesn't produce as many greenhouse gases.

Chapter 3

FARMING MORE WITH LESS

We cannot survive without farms, but we also need healthy natural ecosystems. Plants create the oxygen we breathe. Worms, bugs, and microbes make the soil where plants grow. To reproduce, plants need pollinators such as bees and butterflies. Without pollinators, farmers around the world would have to pay hundreds of billions of dollars to replace the work pollinators do for free.

Butterflies pollinate wild plants, trees, and crops by transferring pollen from one flower to another.

17

To keep Earth's ecosystems healthy, some people think half the planet's land should be devoted to natural habitats. But as the human population grows, we need more land for farms and homes. Scientists and farmers are figuring out ways to grow more food using less space.

Large housing developments leave little room for natural ecosystems or food production.

STEM Spotlight

Scientists are changing the genes in crops so plants have longer roots. This lets them reach deep into the ground for water in dry areas. Genes are like computer code for living things. They help determine how an organism grows, looks, and more. When scientists change genes, they create a genetically modified organism (GMO). Supporters argue GMOs can solve food problems. But critics call GMOs Frankenfoods. They think the changed genes could create unexpected problems for people and the environment.

Scientists try to create GMOs that are stronger, live longer, and produce more food than natural plants do.

VERTICAL FARMING ALLOWS MANY DIFFERENT TYPES OF CROPS TO GROW IN THE SAME SPACE.

The Future of Farms

Someday, most of the vegetables at the grocery store might be grown indoors. In vertical farms, plants are stacked on top of one another on a series of shelves. Farmers can make the environmental conditions inside a vertical farm perfect for plants, even in winter. Vertical farming allows many more plants to grow on an acre (0.4 ha) of land than a traditional farm does.

Soon you may also buy food that grew on the ocean. Water covers about 71 percent of Earth. This isn't a problem for floating farms, or huge barges with multiple levels to produce a variety of foods. The world's first floating farm launched off the coast of the Netherlands in 2018. Machines milk cows as the dairy farm floats on the ocean.

Cows munch on hay on a floating farm in Rotterdam, Netherlands.

Chapter 4

A HEALTHIER FUTURE

Food provides the nutrients and energy we need to survive. Not everything we eat is healthful, though. In the twenty-first century, it's easy to eat food that isn't good for us. Many people have heart disease and other problems caused by the food they eat. Scientists are working on ways to make our food as healthful as possible.

Junk food such as doughnuts is high in fat and sugar and can lead to health problems.

Selective breeding has changed the way crops such as apples look, taste, and feel.

Better Plants

Humans have grown crops for thousands of years. To provide more food for the increasing human population, farmers made crops grow bigger and faster through selective breeding. They allowed only the biggest and fastest-growing plants to grow in their fields.

A scientist reviews the results of a genetic test.

By changing the size of fruits and vegetables, farmers changed the plants' genes. The crops lost some of the genes that led to nutrient production, so modern fruits and vegetables have fewer nutrients than they did thousands of years ago. Scientists are trying to return those lost genes and make fruits and vegetables even healthier.

One of the most nutritious foods is something a lot of us don't eat. Seaweed and other algae are full of nutrients and grow almost anywhere. They could solve many of our food problems. Someday soon, you could be eating algae in your bread, pasta, salads, and even desserts.

Seaweed often has a salty flavor. It can be rubbery or crunchy depending on how it's cooked.

You're Unique, like Everyone Else

For a long time, food scientists told everyone to eat the same things to stay healthy. Modern scientists know that different people react to food in different ways. For example, some people can eat cookies every day without problems. But a daily cookie habit quickly leads to weight gain for others.

Pizza is one of the most popular foods in the United States, but too much of it causes weight gain in some people.

Someday, scientists may study your genes to create a special diet that has all the nutrients you need.

How people react to different foods is determined by their genes, how much they exercise and sleep, and what kinds of microbes live in their gut. In the future, doctors may use this information to determine the best diet for you.

STEM Spotlight

Someday, you might eat food from a printer. A 3D printer can make bread, chocolate, and pasta. It can even print food in fun shapes such as butterflies and dinosaurs. New technology may also help keep you healthy. A monitor on your wrist could test your sweat to see what nutrients your body needs. The monitor could then send the information to a 3D printer that prints food for you containing the needed nutrients.

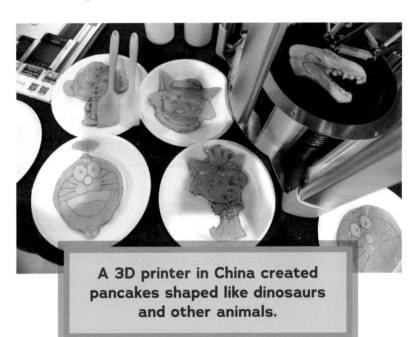

A 3D printer in China created pancakes shaped like dinosaurs and other animals.

Healthy Body, Healthy Planet

We need to provide healthful food for Earth's growing human population while also protecting the planet's ecosystems. Scientists and farmers are rising to the challenge by creating new food and farming technologies. Farms will grow more healthful food and take up less space than ever before. That's good news for both people and the planet.

Cutting-edge farming methods will allow people to eat food that is bigger, healthier, and less harmful to the environment than ever before.

Glossary

alga: plant or plantlike organism

ecosystem: the living and nonliving things that live and interact together in an environment

fertilizer: a substance used to make soil grow more crops

gene: a part of a cell that tells the cell how to grow, look, and act

habitat: the place or environment where a plant or animal naturally or normally lives and grows

livestock: animals such as cows, pigs, and chickens that are raised for food

microbe: a single-celled living thing such as a bacterium

nutrient: a substance a living thing needs to take into its body to grow and survive

pesticide: a chemical used to kill bugs

pollinator: an animal that transfers pollen from one plant to another

selective breeding: changing living things to enhance certain traits in breeding controlled by humans

Learn More about the future of food

Books

Baxter, Roberta. *Bees: Native Pollinators*. Hallandale, FL: EZ Readers, 2019. Learn about different kinds of bees and the important work they do.

Kenney, Karen Latchana. *Cutting-Edge 3D Printing*. Minneapolis: Lerner Publications, 2019. New 3D printing technology can make food, help humans explore space, and much more.

Kurtz, Kevin. *Climate Change and Rising Temperatures*. Minneapolis: Lerner Publications, 2019. Explore Earth's changing climate and what rising temperatures mean for our future.

Websites

Farming Episode—PBS
https://www.pbs.org/video/iptv-kids-clubhouse-iptv-kids-clubhouse-farming-episode/
See the hard work farming takes in this fun video.

My American Farm—Games
http://www.myamericanfarm.org/classroom/games
Visit different farms and play games to learn about the food they produce.

Why Does NASA Care about Food?
https://climatekids.nasa.gov/food/
Find out how NASA uses satellites to help farmers.

Index

Photo Acknowledgments

Image credits: Tetra Images/Getty Images, p. 4; Henry Arden/Getty Images, p. 5; Alexander
Spatari/Getty Images, p. 6; Achim Thomae/Getty Images, p. 7; oticki/Getty Images, p. 8;
bariskaradeniz/Getty Images, p. 9; Vicki Smith/Getty Images, p. 10; Westend61/Getty Images, p. 11;
LauriPatterson/Getty Images, p. 12; istetiana/Getty Images, p. 13; ©fitopardo.com/Getty Images,
p. 14; View Stock/Getty Images, p. 15; chayakorn lotongkum/Getty Images, p. 16; lpweber/Getty
Images, p. 17; dszc/Getty Images, p. 18; Hero Images/Getty Images, pp. 19, 27; LouisHiemstra/
Getty Images, p. 20; Nacho Calonge/Getty Images, p. 21; sara_winter/Getty Images, p. 22;
ljubaphoto/Getty Images, p. 23; TEK IMAGE/Science Photo Library/Getty Images, p. 24;
supermimicry/Getty Images, p. 25; Jose Luis Pelaez Inc/Getty Images, p. 26; Anadolu Agency/
Getty Images, p. 28; Sam Bloomberg-Rissman/Getty Images, p. 29.

Cover: josefkubes/Getty Images.